T0129878

Improve Your English Skills Through
CREATIVE WRITING

Improve Your English Skills Through CREATIVE WRITING

Antony W. Khaemba

authorHOUSE®

AuthorHouse™
1663 Liberty Drive
Bloomington, IN 47403
www.authorhouse.com
Phone: 1 (800) 839-8640

Published by AuthorHouse 11/10/2015

ISBN: 978-1-5049-6059-5 (sc)
ISBN: 978-1-5049-6058-8 (e)

Library of Congress Control Number: 2015918502

Print information available on the last page.

Any people depicted in stock imagery provided by Thinkstock are models, and such images are being used for illustrative purposes only. Certain stock imagery © Thinkstock.

This book is printed on acid-free paper.

Contents

Acknowledgement

*Improve Your English Skills through **Creative Writing*** is dedicated to my mother and mentor Agnes Nekesa Khaemba. Without her guidance, patience, and inspiration, the book would not have been written. All I want My Mom to know is everything I have done I did ultimately for the whole family, I made it mom! I also thank Margaret Njeri Kirumba for her feedback there are no words to express how I feel about you. My friends, brothers and sisters cheers for your encouragement. To My family members you all touch my life no matter the distance. Finally, I thank the staff of Author House for their editorial guidance. I am overwhelmingly grateful.

I also want to thank Elizabeth N khaemba for assisting me put together this book.

Preface

Confessions are tricky. At times as you confess to people you discover valuable lesson about yourself. The journey to writing this book has been lifelong one. I moved from a small village in Kenya to a big city in the United States. I have achieved my dreams and set records that I hope will remain unbroken for a long time. I am ambitious and would like to connect with anyone with a similar joy and goals. Contact me on Facebook look my page (Creative writing) or at E-mail jambilashilla@gmail.com I have been blessed with people who have faith in me. Some have been with me all along others have recently joint me.

I have to thank, above all, God. The blessing that he has showered to me are unbelievable. Thank you God. Without God I would never had made this far.

I guarantee that after you read this book and do all the exercises, your writing skills will improve drastically. Now go for it.

Chapter 1

Creativity and Imagination

Composition writing is all about creating an original and interesting story of your own. You must be creative. To do this, you must decide what to say and how to say it. When you write a essay, you are conveying an idea to somebody who may be far away from you; if you were communicating with someone nearby, you could whisper (or shout). A face-to-face conversation enables you to clarify points, but since the other person (your reader) is not nearby, you must be imaginative enough to sustain the premise. Otherwise, people will get bored and stop reading your work. This is what I mean by *being creative.*

- Step 1: Understand the subject of the story you will write, and choose an appropriate title.
- Step 2: Try to come up with ideas for your story. A good way to do this is to ask yourself as many questions as possible.

Ask Yourself Questions

To be a champion in composition writing, always adopt the "five Ws and one H" method.

- What?
- Where?
- When?
- Who?
- Why?
- How?

For example, let's say I have been tasked with writing an essay about my school. To spark my creativity, I might ask myself the following questions. Note how they all begin with one of the action words I have listed above.

- What is the name of the school?
- Where is it located?
- When was it established?
- Why was it built in that particular area?
- Who heads it?
- What can I say about the teachers?
- What can I say about the other staff?
- What does the physical facility look like?

- How do students fare in exams?
- What about extracurricular activities?
- What do I like about my school?
- What is the school motto?
- What problems, if any, affect our school?
- How does the school address these problems?
- How are the parents? Are they cooperative?
- How does the school help the local community?
- What can I say about some specific boys and girls?
- What are the hopes of the students?

Once I have the answers to my questions, I can write my story. There are so many questions I might ask myself; the list above is just the beginning.

Assignment 1
Write an essay about a football match at your school. Here are some questions you might ask yourself before you begin:

- When and where was the match held?
- Why was that particular venue chosen?
- Which teams played?
- What were the most exciting moments?
- How did the spectators react?
- Which team won?
- How was the victory celebrated?
- How did the referee do?

Note: In most national examinations in Kenya, the examiner is likely to assign you an essay that has something to do with football. This is because most schools have football pitches. Since students may not have any experience with other sports, it wouldn't make sense to ask them to write about rugby or hockey or basketball. However, students should be familiar with the rules of netball and volleyball.

Assignment 2
Write an essay about a disappointing exchange at the market. Here are some questions you might ask yourself:

- What is the name of the market?
- Where is it?
- Which day is market day?
- Why did you go there?
- Why was the transaction disappointing?
- What could you have done differently?
- Where do the traders come from?
- Who are the buyers?
- What products are sold?
- How busy is market day?

- How long does the market remain open?
- How are goods arranged?
- What problems are there?
- How are those problems resolved?

Assignment 3

Write an essay about a dream you've had. Here are some questions you might ask yourself:

- What did you dream about?
- How did you behave in the dream?
- How did the dream make you feel? Excited? Frightened?
- How did you wake up?
- What did you feel when you realized it was just a dream?
- What events or thoughts do you think led to the dream?

Note: Many writers will let readers know from the start that the story is about a dream. Consider how much more interesting it will be if readers realize it on their own as the story comes to an end. For example, don't use a sentence like this in your writing:

> When I was sleeping, I dreamt that a monster was moving at a supersonic speed toward me.

Instead, try this approach:

> That night, I went to bed rather late. Suddenly, a stranger appeared. He was walking slowly, his large head held high on his strong neck and huge shoulders. He paced up and down the room with a whip held tightly in his left hand, and he repeatedly threatened to whip me if I did not explain where the gold was!

The second example creates suspense by keeping secret the fact that the protagonist is dreaming. Here is an example of a good ending:

> The lion was more focused on me than on my younger brother, so I jumped over the fence and tried to escape through the main gate. As the monster opened its mouth to swallow me, I felt a hand pulling me. It was my mother waking me up for school. When I opened my eyes, I could not believe I had been dreaming. I remembered what had happened so vividly. I tried to call to my brother in the next room, but no sound came out. I was terrified and remained in my bed.

Assignment 4

Write about what you want to be when you grow up. For example, your dream might be to become a doctor. Here are some questions you might ask yourself:

- What do you enjoy doing?
- How can you get a job in this field?
- Why do you want to pursue this interest?
- What are the benefits of working in this field?

- What sort of training will you need?
- What sort of medicine will you pursue?
- Why do you want to be a doctor?

Assignment 5

Write an essay about your best friend. Here are some questions you might ask:

- Who is your friend?
- Where does your friend come from?
- Who are your friend's parents?
- Where does your friend go to school?
- When did you become friends?
- What do you like most about your friend?
- What does your friend like most about you?
- What does your friend do to make you laugh?
- What funny things has your friend done?
- What things do you do together?
- When do you visit each other's homes?
- What do you plan to do together in future?
- Why do you think it is important to have a friend?

It's also important to include realistic conflict in your writing; even the best friends disagree from time to time. Describing how you and your best friend fought and reconciled will make your story much more interesting. Here are some questions you might ask:

- Why did you and your best friend fight?
- What made you angry at this other person?
- What challenges (opposition from your parents, scheduling issues, living far apart, etc.) have you faced as friends?
- How did you reconcile?

Comments

When you are writing about your best friend, even if you are describing a disagreement, be compassionate. Never forget that you are writing about a friend, not an enemy (unless it is your goal to turn your friend into an enemy). This does not mean you can't write a negative sentence or two; even the best friend has bad days. In this case, explain that it was only a day and that the bad blood was there for only a short time. You can use popular sayings to explain the situation. It's also a good idea to include this sort of information in the middle of your story. For example:

> After the fight with John, I declared that I would never ever talk to him again. But he came and asked me for forgiveness. I changed my mind, forgot all about the fight, and forgave him. As the saying goes, "To err is human; to forgive, divine."

Describe the person, inside and out. Give a real picture of your friend. In the description below, the writer describes body type, skin, and hair color—the most striking features of his best friend, the ones that make her different than other people. Such a description makes a person more realistic to readers.

Mary is my best friend; she will celebrate her fifteenth birthday this year. She has lovely brown skin and black hair, and she lives with her parents. Her father is a farmer and grows maize. She speaks English and Swahili fluently. She is short and stout.

Assignment 6
Write an essay about what makes your country better than any other. Here are some questions you might ask yourself:

- Why do you think your country is the best country?
- What are the defining features of your country's landscape?
- How are people treated in your country?
- Why should people visit your country?
- What misconceptions about your country can you correct?

The Power of Outlining
In addition to asking yourself questions, you can also use an outline to keep your composition organized and on task. If you don't know where to start, first write down everything that comes to mind. Once you've done that, you can then reorganize the ideas in a more logical order.

Sample Outline: The Importance of Trees
Provide wood for

- furniture
- fuel
- buildings

Provide food

- feed for animals
- fruit for people

Used in agriculture to

- prevent soil erosion
- provide shade
- fertilize the soil
- act as windbreakers

Other uses:

- Medicinal value, e.g., *"mwarubaini"*
- Home for wildlife and birds
- Religious value, e.g., shrines
- Attract rain
- Paper industry
- Beautiful scenery that attracts tourist.

Assignment 7
Expand on the points outlined above, and write a composition on the importance of trees.

Sample Outline: Wildlife Has Many Benefits
Advantages

- Enhances economic development by attracting tourists, supporting hotel development, and creating job opportunities
- Promotes international relationships
- Interesting to watch
- Food source
- Skin, hooves, etc., used in industry

Disadvantages

- Attacks people and livestock
- Destroys crops and farm land
- Decreases land available for human settlement.
- Encourages corrupt practices, e.g., poaching

Assignment 8
Expand on the points listed above, and write a composition that explains that there are more advantages than disadvantages to wildlife. In your discussion, list the pros and cons, the advantages and disadvantages. Think of your essay like a debate. The best way to discuss the topic is to start with the advantages and then describe the disadvantages. In your last paragraph, state that there are more advantages than disadvantages.

Sample Outline: Causes and Prevention of HIV/AIDS
Causes

- Sexual intercourse with an infected person
- Unsafe blood transfusion
- Unsafe injections
- Sharing cutting or piercing instruments like razor blades or needles
- Open wounds and cuts
- Transferred from infected mother to unborn baby
- Breast feeding

Prevention

- Abstain from sexual intercourse before marriage.
- Be faithful to your spouse.
- Only get a blood transfusion in a reputable hospital.
- Avoid cutting the skin or piecing the ear with unsafe instruments.

Other comments

- As yet, there is no cure for HIV/AIDS.
- It can infect anyone.
- It can kill anyone.

Note: HIV/AIDS is a national disaster in Kenya; a lot of people are dying from the disease. The Kenya National Examinations Council is likely to ask pupils to write an essay on this topic. It might be this year.

Assignment 9
Write an essay about HIV/AIDS. Include the things that cannot lead to infections in other people, e.g., kissing, sharing the same plate of food, sharing clothes, etc.

Composition Elements
You may be given one of the following elements and be asked to develop a composition:

(a) introduction (or beginning)
(b) conclusion (or ending)
(c) composites(or the middle)

Assignment 10a
Example: Introduction
The sentences below are the beginning of a story. Read them carefully, and then complete the story making it as interesting as possible. Remember: this will be a happy story, because the mother is excited.

> That day my mother came home unusually early. Looking excited, she called all of us into the sitting room. When we were all seated,_____

_____

_____

Assignment 10b
Example: Conclusion
Write a story ending in the words below. Make your story as interesting as you can. Describe a memorable day, one that is either extremely exciting or extremely horrifying.

> ....
> ....
> That was a day I will not forget for a long time to come.

Assignment 10c
Example: Composition Based on a Proverb
Write a story that shows the truth in the proverb "hurry, hurry has no blessing." Let the proverb serve as the title of the essay.

Assignment 10d
Write an essay about the proverb "slow and steady wins the race." Make sure you fully understand the meaning of the proverb before you start.

Sample Essays
Below are examples of student-written compositions, written by several pupils in different schools. They are followed by suggestions of what might be done to improve the essay.

"Adventures in the Forest": Original Version

She had now been walking for almost two hours. Suddenly Elizabeth stepped still. Did she hear noise in the forest or a roar! Is it her imagination? She listened again and there came a scream of a baby, then of roar like that of a lion and abruptly everything subsided to quietness
Elizabeth stood astonished. Her mind was filled with thousands of thoughts. She tried to concentrate to ring one thought into focus but was not futile. She decided to take to her heels.

Suddenly, there were laughter's of many people coming from the forest. The laughter's were as if the people were enjoying themselves. They were cheering and jeering. Then it came again; the scream of a baby. This time round more loudly. She crotched to catch the voice clearly and if possible identify it. In a split of a seconds went the roar again it seemed to be approaching where Elizabeth was.

Elizabeth was a young girl she was had been waiting to celebrate her sixteenth birthday. She had always been imagining how she would be looking like when she clocked sixteen. She was beautiful she knew it and at sixteen, she figured out that she will be more beautiful. Her face was wide, with fleshy lips and her eyes were clearly as brown as those ones of a newly born baby. She had a dream in life and knew that if she did not save herself, then everything would spill.

Her body was shivering from extreme fear. Her heart beats were almost audible. The hair on her head stood still, she tried again to run but her thin legs could not carry her due to fear. It was as if there was o connection between her body and legs.

"A child crying, a roar" what is the meaning of this" she thought a loud. While she was still pondering about the mystery she was hard hit from behind! She rolled and fell down with a thud "puu-up"

Since she had heard stories of wild animal which did not feast on dead carcass, she pretended to be dead. She held up her breath as the animals rounded her licking her. Then the animals a lion, may be, was sure that Elizabeth was dead. It went away. For all this time she did not open her eyes." Thank you God" she said as she made her way out of the forest.

8

Comments

I would have given this essay 20 marks out of 40 possible point The writer made some foolish mistakes on tenses and sentence structure. Sentence structure is all about arranging your words in a logical manner to give sense. One way to learn about sentence structure is to read a lot of storybooks. The writer would have used words that are attractive to attract the examiner.

Here is the composition again, with some additional flavor that could have been added to each paragraph.

"Adventures in the Forest": Rewritten Version

At first, Elizabeth thought her mind was playing tricks on her. But everything was as quiet as a grave. Then she smelt a rat, as the saying goes. Clouds indicated rain. Instinctively, she realized something was wrong. She had been walking for almost two hours. Suddenly Elizabeth stood still. She'd heard a noise in the forest. Was that a roar? Was it her imagination? She listened again and heard the scream of a baby, then a roar like that of a lion. Abruptly, everything went quiet.

She faced a dilemma; she was as confused as a rat caught red-handed in the kitchen. She wished the earth would open up and swallow her. She thought of running for her life, but Elizabeth stood there, astonished. Her mind was filled with a thousand thoughts. She tried to concentrate, to bring one thought into focus, but it was futile. She decided to take to her heels.

Suddenly, she heard laughter from many people; the laughter came from the forest. The people sounded as if they were enjoying themselves. They were cheering and jeering. When she heard people cheering, her heart leapt into her month. Instinctively, she crouched down and did not move. She was caught between a rock and a hard place. Then it came again: the scream of a baby, this time, more loudly. She crouched so she could hear the voice clearly and, if possible, identify it. A split second later, she heard the roar again. It seemed to be approaching Elizabeth.

Elizabeth was a young girl who was about to celebrate her sixteenth birthday. She had always imagined what she would look like when she reached sixteen. She was beautiful, and she knew it. She figured that at sixteen she would be even more beautiful. Her face was wide, with full lips, and her eyes were brown. She knew she had to save herself. She thought about escaping to a place where there were people and buildings. She had to move quickly; as the saying goes, a man can be saved at the eleventh hour. Elizabeth "died" every time she heard the roar.

Her body was shaking like a hen that had been dipped in cold water, like a papyrus reed on a windy day. Her heartbeats were almost audible. Danger loomed ahead. The hair on her head stood still, she tried again to run but her thin legs could not carry her due to fear. It was as if there was no connection between her body and legs. Her day of reckoning was near.

The roar turned into a lion, which was roaring furiously. Elizabeth quickly said her last prayer; she knew that the next few seconds she would kick the bucket. She pleaded with her Creator to save her; she believed she was experiencing her last seconds on Earth. She knew death was inevitable and coming very fast. "A child crying. A roar. What is the meaning of this?" she said aloud. Suddenly, a kick from behind made her stumble, lose her balance, and fall to the ground with a thud.

She had heard that wild animals did not feast on dead carcasses, so she pretended to be dead. She held her breath as the animal—she thought it was a lion—circled her, licking her. When it was sure Elizabeth was dead, it went away. Perhaps the lion knew the old saying: a watched pot never boils. She did not open her eyes until she was sure it had gone. "Thank you, God," she said, as she made her way out of the forest.

Assignment 11

Write an essay about an adventure in the forest using the "composition flavors" listed below. Incorporate the below set of "composition Flavors" in your essay.

- She heard a noise in the forest, or was it a roar?
- suddenly there were peals of laughter, which seemed to come from a group of people deep in the forest
- then it came again: the unmistakable scream of a baby
- she was consumed by fear, shivering and trembling like a twig in a storm
- hairs on her skin stood erect like a company of soldiers
- she tried to run, but her weak legs let her down
- it is true what they say: where there is a will, there is a way
- she had cheated death

"A Strange Encounter": Original Version

I. An old man appeared at our gate we went out to meet him. His already lined face creased into a smile when he heard us. It was a distinguished face full of wisdom. We stretched our hands to greet him just to discover that he was blind eeh!

II. He had shaggy hair. His distinguished face from appearance seemed to have been very handsome during his youth-full days. His smile revealed no tooth and as my sister and I patted him at the back to reassure him that we understood his nature he said "hallow!" expressing his teethlessness.

III. He was on a patched, dark coat. His shirt was dirty and the collar was black may be due to prolonged usage without changing. His trousers were dark and worn out. The shoes had hole revealing his ugly toes.

IV. We welcomed him to the house offered him a seat and a glass of water. Pleased with our hospitality and warm welcome he fell free and started revealing his story to us.

V.   He said that he had come a long way looking for a person. The person he was looking for has roots in a village in the north where the old man hails from the directions and descriptions the place he was directed to fits our place of dwelling.

VI.   The old man was known as Musa; alone name. He had no other name "The person I am looking for was born in a family of two. Him and his brother "The old man explained; one day the two brothers had gone to the market. After finishing their copping, they started their way back home. On the way came a dogs and they started running after them. They were astonished at the action of the dogs since they were only twelve years old.

VII. Were they were young, they became frightened and they took to their heels? They became frightened and took to their heels. They decided each to go to his direction to confuse the dogs." Yes they did confuse the dogs but they never found each other gain!" he said this statement with a heavy heart, and tears rolling down his chicks.

VIII. The other brother found himself in a strange place with strange people! He had a lot of problems since no one was there to help him. One day he saw a truck leaving the village. He sneaked into the truck and hid between cartons that were loaded inside the truck, hoping against fate he will be back at his home village.

IX.   Fate did not favor him. The truck used to travel far deep into the south village. As a result he was moved further a way from his home village! From there it becomes impossible for him to locate his home. After a long period of trying and failing, he despaired and decided to live there.

X.   The old man picked up the glass of water sipped it then he cleared his throat "yesterday this story was broadcaster over the Radio" The old man proceeded; my heart skipped a bit as the man said these.

XI.   The person who went to the south is my son! He paused to swallow saliva. "The description given over the radio seemed here" The lost son had given the description of where he had finally settled. Following the description, I decided to trace the place so I don't know if I have finally reached? The old man concluded his touching story by asking us the question.

XII. It was like a dream. The person happened to be our father and therefore the man sited next to me was my grandfather, life can at times be interesting. if not funny!

"A Strange Encounter": Rewritten Version

An old man appeared at our gate. We went out to meet him. As the saying goes, old is gold. His lined face creased into a smile. It was a distinguished face, full of wisdom. We stretched our hands to greet him and discovered that he was blind. Eeh! I was flabbergasted to find out he was blind. We entered the house, and I banged the door behind us.

He shifted the bundle he was carrying from his left hand to his right. He had shaggy hair. His distinguished face suggested that he had been very handsome during his youth. His smile revealed that he had no teeth. My sister and I patted his back to reassure him that we understood his nature, and he said "Hello!"

He wore a patched, dark coat. His shirt was dirty, and the collar was black, maybe due to prolonged usage without changing. His trousers were dark and worn out. The shoes had holes that revealed his ugly toes.

We welcomed him to the house and offered him a seat and a glass of water. Pleased with our hospitality and warm welcome, he felt comfortable and told us his story.

He said he had come a long way and was looking for a person from his hometown, a village in the north. His description fit the place where we lived.

The old man was known only as Musa. He had no other name. "The person I am looking for had one brother," the old man explained. One day, the two brothers had gone to the market. After they finished their shopping, they made their way back home. On the way, dogs started running after them. The boys were astonished; they were only twelve years old.

When the dogs appeared, the boys took off, as fast as lighting. Frightened, they ran as though their lives depended on it. They decided to go in different directions to confuse the dogs. Unfortunately, the two boys never saw each other again. The old man said this with a heavy heart, and tears rolled down his cheeks, like water flowing down a mountain.

One brother found himself in a strange place with strange people. He had a lot of problems, since no one was there to help him. He lived hand to mouth. One day he saw a truck leaving the village. He snuck onto the truck and hid between some cartons inside, hoping it would return him to his home village.

Luck was not with him. His effort to find his home was as successful as an attempt to milk a hen. The truck traveled deep into the south. As a result, he moved further away from his home village! It became impossible for him to locate his home. After a long period of trying and failing, he despaired and decided to live in the southern village. He made the best out of a bad situation.

The old man picked up a glass of water and sipped it. Then he cleared his throat. "Yesterday this story was broadcast over the radio," he said. My heart skipped a bit as the man spoke his next words.

"The person who went to the south is my son!" He swallowed. "The description given over the radio sent me here." The lost son had described the place where he had finally settled. "I decided to find the place," the old man said. "Have I finally reached it?" The old man concluded his touching story.

We were all silent as we listened to him. It was like a dream. The lost son happened to be our father, and therefore the man sitting next to me was my grandfather. I almost jumped out of my skin; my heart beat like a drum. Life at times can be interesting, if not funny! I assured the old man that he had reached his destination, and he was as proud as a peacock. He said the search for his son had been looking for a pin in the sea. He was like a barren woman who had finally conceived.

Assignment 12
Identify the spelling, punctuation, and grammatical mistakes in the original version of this composition.

Assignment 13
Write an essay about an encounter with a long-lost friend.

"A Road Accident": Original Version

I.   I remember very well that black Sunday morning when I left to pay my aunt a visit that stays at Turbo. Since I had been to the place before, I did not need any company. From home to the buss stop is not far so I was soon there.

II.   No sooner had I arrived than I saw a bus a way on the hill. The bus-stop was located on the left side of the road. The sun was above me, its rays penetrated the clouds and hit the innocent ground so arrogantly. I took refuge in a shady shed I could see the bus climbing the hill to the top.

III. Since the hill was so steep the road had been constructed on a spiral manner. This was to cut down the force need to climb the steep hill. As a result, of this the other side of the road ran down the steep slope.

IV.   The bus was approaching slowly, it was smoking heavily behind it and the engine produced unusual sound. Then the bus came past the stage, I thought the bus was supposed to slow down in a way of stopping. Instead it grew fast and faster.

V.   My surprise rose to an alarm when the passengers started crying for help. I straight away knew the bus was out of control. The bus headed straight to another shed on the other side of the road. People were inside the shade too. They were quick to react, they squeezed in one corner as if they could go through the walls of the shed.

VI.   To open and close the eyes, the bus flew high into the air. Then it made a turn in the air. The huge bus seemed as light as feather scream of agony rented the air. Suddenly the debris bus once beautiful landed on the bare ground with a loud bang "mbu-upp!"

VII. I stood horrified. I did not expect such a calamity. I wondered if I was watching a film! But no the reality was the bus had rolled. It had been blown off completely. It's once time rectangular nice shape had been seriously damage!

VIII. Apparently this is the bus I was supposing to board. I turned my face away from the sight and stared at the sky as if I was praying. A couple of minutes passed I turned to face the sight, so slowly, anticipating may be not to see the bus there. But the bus was there!

IX.   I recollected my minds and rushed down the hill to save the survivors but suddenly fire sprung. The smoke rose high in the sky. There was an explosion throwing pieces of metals and other materials igniting up in the sky. Somebody from the crown raised his voice and said "Do not move closer, it dangerous!"

X.   was nothing I could do! I stood there looking at the bus helplessly as the inferno reduced it into ashes. To me, it was worse. I felt like I could have helped.

Comments

I would award the composition above 28 or 29 marks. It describes a terrible event. The writer could have showed how bad the accident was by using emotion. There are a few spelling mistakes; dictionaries can help pupils improve their spelling. The composition also lacks descriptive text, such as similes; it is very plain. Pupils are advised to choose words that will appeal to the examiner. See below for a suggested rewrite.

"A Road Accident": Rewritten Version

One Sunday morning, I paid a visit to my aunt in Turbo. Since I had been to the place before, I did not need anyone to accompany me. I planned to take the bus. The bus stop is not far from my home, so I was soon there.

As soon as I arrived, I saw a bus coming up the hill. I heard the rattling of the engine as it moved at a snail's pace. The bus stop was on the left side of the road. The sun was above me; its rays penetrated the clouds and hit the ground hard. I took refuge in a shady shed.

Since the hill was so steep, the road had been constructed in a spiral manner. This cut down on the force a vehicle needed to climb the hill. But it meant cars going in the other direction had to go down a steep slope.

The bus approached slowly, smoking heavily. The engine made an unusual sound. I'd thought the bus would slow down when it neared the stop. Instead, it stopped and rolled back down the hill, moving faster and faster.

My surprise changed to alarm when the passengers started crying for help. I realized the bus was out of control. It headed straight toward a shed on the other side of the road. The people inside reacted quickly, squeezing into one corner as if they could go through the walls.

The bus flew high and seemed to make a turn in the air. The huge bus seemed as light as feather. A scream of agony went through the air. Suddenly the bus landed on the bare ground with a loud bang. There were bodies lying in the road. People were yelling and screaming.

I stood there, horrified. I had not expected such a calamity. I thought I was watching a film! But no, it was reality. The bus was completely blown apart. Its once rectangular shape was seriously damaged.

This was the bus I was supposed to board. I turned my face away from the sight and stared at the sky as if I were praying. A couple of minutes passed. I turned back slowly, hoping that I would not see the bus. But there it was!

I collected my thoughts, found some courage, and rushed down the hill to help the survivors. Suddenly a fire ignited; smoke rose high. An explosion threw pieces of metal and other materials into the sky. Somebody raised his voice and said, "Do not move closer. It is dangerous!" The bus burst into flames. There was no hope of rescuing anyone.

There was nothing I could do. I stood there, looking at the bus as the fire reduced it into ashes. I felt terrible, because I thought I could have helped.

"Fishing Turns Sour": Original Version

I.   There was thunder and lightening prior to a heavy rainfall. The lake had changed to an irregular wavy like folds. The wind was blowing violently. From the middle of the lake my father and I could see tiny vegetation which was meant to be trees at the beach.

II. We had been fishing the whole night. We had made a good catch and so we were returning home before it started raining. We were in a boat trying effortlessly to keep ourselves on top of the rough lake. One second we were on top of the wave, and the other second found us down. We were so much trying to keep the water out of the boat and fighting to row the boat to the show line. The lake had changed into a "beast"

III. The clouds had come down forming a layer of fog which could not be penetrated by our naked eyes. The wind grew strong and stronger each minute, the situation became worst. The waves were unbearable. My father was freezing cold, is teeth chattering against each other as if in a bottle to knock each other out of position.

IV. I was dripping with sweat as a matter of panic. We kept the pot boiling by fighting to save the boat from capsizing. To me it was a fight to save the boat from being sabotaged by the demons deep in the lake. I wanted, to emerge the winner so I fought harder as the saying goes: nothing comes on a silver platter.

V.   "Who can battle with water?" Despaired my father" It does not feel pain neither doe it get tired. It comes as if it does not care, neither afraid" "The old man lamented. He preceded with a choking voice "My son dive and swim and try to save your life. I am old. My days are few I can die here!" I could not believe what my ears heard. I felt like giving him a slap but instead, gave him one of my wildest smiles of reassurance.

VI. The wave was again strong, like a blow of a ghost. The water rose again, coming down and up, again and again. The boat rocked on it. It moved up and down as if dancing to its tune.

VII. I found myself holding a piece of timber my head aching like hell. My whole body ached too as if stung by wild bees. I tried to gather thoughts. "Yah! I was in a boat" Then again I was in the air. Suddenly I went like a heavy stone into the shallow water.

VIII. I rose up. The water was at waist height. I tried to move my legs toward the shallow end, but they felt like heavy stone to lift. I was hurt, but could not spare any chances. This was a matter of life and death.

IX. I found my self swimming. Luckily enough, I was a good swimmer and knew many ways of swimming. I am not a coward as the saying goes cowards die many time before their real death. I swam for a while and found myself on a dry land! Then I felt dizzy and fell asleep.

X. I woke up in the midst of mourning people. My mother was screaming wildly, as if she would be paid for that. My brothers too filled the air with cries" where is your dad? "Inquired my mother."

Comments

This essay might be awarded 30 to 32 marks. The writer incorporates dialogue between the son and father in the fifth paragraph, which brings the essay to life. The opening and closing quote marks are used to show the exact words spoken by speakers. The quote marks around the word "beast" indicate that the lake seemed to have animal-like behavior. Words in a language other than English can also put into quotes or underlined. Here is a suggested rewrite.

"Fishing Turns Sour" Rewritten Version

My father and I were in a boat in the middle of the lake. There was thunder and lightning suggested a heavy rainfall was on its way. The waves on the lake were irregular and looked like folds of cloth. The wind blew violently. We could see tiny vegetation in the distance, which was actually trees on the beach. The trees seemed to gather around each other as if they were participating in a meeting called by Satan to overthrow God.

During the holidays, I would help my aging father when he went fishing. We had been fishing the whole night. We'd made a good catch, and so we decided to head home before it started raining. We tried to keep our boat afloat in the rough lake. One second we were on top of the wave, and the next one found us down. We tried hard to keep the water out of the boat and row it to the shoreline. But the "beast" had other plans. Fishing is a bed of roses when the lake is calm. But on this day, the wind was like a thorn in our flesh; it would not allow us to row the boat smoothly.

The clouds formed a layer of fog that our eyes could not penetrate. They covered the ocean like a blanket. The wind grew stronger and stronger each minute; the situation got worse. The waves were unbearable. My father was freezing cold; his teeth chattered against each other so much, I thought they'd knock themselves out of his mouth. I remembered the biblical story of Noah and thought God had decided to finish us using water.

I was dripping with sweat; I was in a panic. We fought to keep the boat from capsizing. I felt as though I was fighting to save the boat from demons deep in the lake. I wanted to win, so I fought harder. As they say, nothing comes on a silver platter.

"Who can battle against water?" My father was in despair. "It does not feel pain or get tired. It does not care or feel fear." The old man's voice seemed to choke. "My son," he said, "dive and swim and try to save your life. I am old. My days are few. I can die here!" I could not believe what my ears were hearing. I wanted to give him a slap, but instead I gave him a smile of reassurance.

The water rose and fell again, up and down, again and again. The boat rocked on it, moving up and down as if it were dancing to a tune.

I held onto a piece of timber; my head and my whole body ached like hell, as if I'd been stung by wild bees. I tried to gather my thoughts. Then, one minute I was in a boat, and the next I was in the air. Suddenly, I went like a heavy stone into the shallow water. My great-grandparents were right when they said misfortune knocks once at every man's door.

I stood up. The water came up to my noise. I tried to move my legs toward the shore, but they felt like heavy stones. I was hurt but could not take any chances. This was a matter of life and death.

I started swimming. Luckily enough, I was a good swimmer. I am not a coward; there is a saying: cowards die many times before their real death. I swam for a while and found myself on dry land. I felt dizzy and fell asleep.

I was rushed to the hospital and treated by the tender hands of a nurse. I woke up surrounded by mourning people. My mother was screaming wildly, and my brothers filled the air with cries. "Where is your dad?" asked my mother. I swore to God that I would never return to the lake again.

Assignment 14
Write an essay about a horrifying car accident or a good day that goes bad. Begin with an outline, using the "five Ws and one H" method.

"Good News Turns Sour": Original Version

I.   It was late in the day and the sun was settings. Its faded orange rays could be seen just above the horizon. The narrow path was darkening, it was a moonless night. The narrow path was darkening. It was then said that the moon had gone go consult its "husband" the sun before coming back. Darkness was approaching faster. I was worried. On each side of the narrow foot path was thick bushes in which wizards hid at night to frighten late comers from the local market.

II.   Suddenly I heard shouts of "thief! Thief! The thief made his way to the grave yards clutching his bag he thought he was cleaver to hide his valuables in cemetery because people are afraid of burial places especially at night. Yes its cleaver to do so and indeed people are afraid of such sites, but being at a loose end, the villager had no alternative than to play a hero and pursu the man to whenever he could go.

III.   The thief was quit a head of the crowd he manages to disappear beyond darkness and varnished into the thin air armed to the teeth with the stolen bag.

IV.   The bag had precious ornament stolen from a village business lady by the name Hope. She had wealth. She owned a big plot in the village where she had put up her grand house that looked like a king's palace. No one knew how the thief had made his way into the house because the house was believed to be extremely secured with all doors under key and lock always.

V.   Having lost so much the village tycoon offered to give a quarter of the stolen wealth to whoever got the bag back. It was a tempting offer. Everybody was ready to make sure he or she was the one to get the bag.

VI.   The cemetery was dark from where I stood I could only see darkness around me as if I was surrounded by walls of blackness. I was frightened and each sound made me turn abruptly at its direction. The wind blew gently making the trees in the grave yard bend as if obeying some given command. The motion of the tree made shadows in the darkness that molded themselves to fearfully forms.

VII.   "Diamond means so much and gold means much more. To get the bag is to achieve wealth and nothing comes easily" said Hope so the severe condition meant nothing to us. The search started, "looking for a bag," in the cemetery! We were in a team but working in disunity. Everybody hoping against odds to get the bag by himself or herself. I was also busy searching.

VIII.   Then I was pricked by a rose flower on my right foot. It felt so painful. I bent down to remove the thorn. My face then landed on a black object; instead I touched it. It was the leather bag. I picked it up and shouted "I have got it!"

IX.   There were sounds of feet thumbs coming towards me. Then from my front rose a figure from nowhere! Its face was masked. He grabbed the bag from me. He with draw something from his pockets and hit me on my face I slumped down to the ground.

X.   As the figure made frantic efforts to escape and hide, the crowd had already reached. It was too late. He was overpowered and beaten. The mask was removed as the figure bled profusely. To the surprise of the crowd and Hope it was Hope's eldest son! what dramatic turn of events l thought as hope's son was being unmasked

"Good News Turns Sour": Rewritten Version

It was late in the day, and the sun was setting. Its faded orange rays could be seen just above the horizon. The narrow path was dark; it was a moonless night. The moon had gone to consult her husband, the sun. I was worried. On each side of the narrow footpath were thick bushes where wizards hid at night to frighten latecomers from the local market.

Suddenly I heard shouts of "Thief! Thief!" Someone ran to the graveyard, clutching a bag. Clearly, he thought he was clever to hide his valuables in cemetery, because people are afraid of burial places, especially at night. The villager had no alternative but to play the hero and pursue the man wherever he went.

The thief was quite ahead of the crowd. He managed to disappear into the darkness and into the thin air, still carrying the stolen bag.

The bag contained a valuable ornament, stolen from a businesswoman named Hope. She was wealthy. She owned a big plot of land in the village, where she had built a grand house that looked like a king's palace. No one knew how the thief had gotten into the house, because it was believed to be extremely secure, with all the doors always locked.

The businesswoman offered a quarter of the value of the stolen ornament to whoever got the bag back. It was a tempting offer. Everyone wanted to make sure that he or she got the bag.

The cemetery was dark. From where I stood, I could see only darkness around me. I was surrounded by walls of blackness. I was frightened, and each sound made me jump. The wind made the trees in the graveyard bend as if they were obeying someone's command. The tree shadows took on frightful forms.

"Diamonds mean so much, and gold means much more," said Hope. "To get the bag is to achieve wealth, and it will not come easily." The difficult conditions did not worry us. We started to search for the bag in the cemetery! We were a team, but each one was working for himself or herself. Everybody hoping against odds to get the bag, including me.

I stepped on a rose stem with my right foot. It was very painful. I bent down to remove the thorn. My eyes landed on a black object, which I touched. It was the leather bag. I picked it up and shouted, "I have got it!"

Footsteps ran toward me. In front of me a figure rose from nowhere. His face was masked. He grabbed the bag from me. He withdrew something from his pockets and hit me in my face. I slumped down to the ground. A feeling of joy went through me. I knew my life had taken a new turn. I was going to buy a plot of land and build a new house. Without wasting a second, I asked Hope for my reward.

In the meantime, the masked figure made a frantic effort to escape and hide, but the crowd was already near, and they surrounded him. It was too late for him. He was overpowered and beaten. He bled profusely as they removed the mask. To everyone's surprise, it was Hope's eldest son! What dramatic turn of events!

Assignment 15
Write an essay that shows that good news sometimes can be accompanied by something negative.

"Confused in the Morning": Original Version

I. The sun was already up by the time I woke up. All of a sudden I remembered what I was supposed to do. I skipped out of the bed, picked my watch and gazed at it for a couple of moments as if I did not perceive what I was observing "Ten o'clock, yes ten o'clock! Heard myself whisper "what is the meaning of ten o'clock, you fool! I screamed "it is tenth October you fool".

II. I bent as if my hips had a hinge, pulled out my leather shoes and rushed my feet inside them as if the shoes would respond in the same manner. These actions happened automatically one would think I had been connected to an electric switch which had been turned on!

III. No sooner had I stuck the shoe on my feet than I realized I was in my pajama I pulled the shoes in an effort to remove them, but I could removed them prior hurting my lips against the kneecap.

IV. I rushed to the wardrobe sorted my suits picked a stripped brown one and pulled it up my things in a manner of waving. I grabbed a white shirt rapped it around my back as my arms made their way through the long sleeves and then went back to my shoes.

V. Immediately I had put on my shoes, I realized I was supposed to have worn the socks first "Oh God! I heard myself matter. I decided to forget about the socks!.

VI. I tiptoed towards the bathroom. Inside I ran a stream of water on my head. The water was pinching with coldness. I took a towel ran it on my hair and face so fast that the joints of my arms twisted in pain. I grabbed oil and rubbed it against my face and hair a simultaneously I picked a comb and ran it through my hair.

VII. I was already late. I had less than one minutes to run to the bus stop and pick a bus to an interview. The interview was being conducted fifteen kilometers from my place of dwelling. I had eagerly waited for this day and late night I did not sleep I kept on turning and tossing about on bed curiously thinking of how life would be changed. If I landed that job will buy a car, build a palace, save a lot. I had built castle in the air.

VIII.   It was late, I knew, but I had to make it up because I had been waiting for the day. I had been as patient as a farmer waiting for the harvesting season. And the day had reached.

IX.   I looked on the mirror, and my image was not fascinating at all. I smiled to remove the creases on my face, but instead I looked more miserable. I did not brush my teeth I prayed so as God would take care of me.

X.   Picked my certificates and as I made my way through the door, my eyes ran over the calendar tenth October is supposed to be a Friday. Today is a Thursday" Alas! Exclaimed as I made a step back and looked more clearly. It is ninth October what a fool I had made of me. My eyes remained glued to the calendar an if it had been dropped straight from the sky. I felt like screaming with laughter but, my body so tired that I sat down and rested.

Comments
Parts of the composition can describe how people get ready after they wake up.

"Confused in the Morning": Rewritten Version

The sun was already up by the time I woke up. All of a sudden I remembered what I was supposed to do. I skipped out of the bed and picked up my watch. I gazed at it for a couple of minutes, as if I did not understand what I was seeing. "Ten o'clock, yes, ten o'clock," I whispered. "What is the meaning of ten o'clock?" Then I screamed. "You fool! It is the tenth of October!"

I bent as if my hips had a hinge, pulled out my leather shoes, and pushed my feet inside them. My actions were so automatic, one would think I was a robot.

As soon as I stuck the shoes on my feet, I realized I was in my pajamas. I pulled off the shoes to remove my pajamas.

I rushed to the wardrobe, looked through my suits, and picked one with brown stripes. I searched for a shirt, but there was none in the wardrobe. I remembered that I had a clean, white one in my briefcase. I grabbed it and put it on. Then I went back to my shoes.

Again, I put on my shoes. Then I realized I needed socks. "Oh God!" I muttered and decided to forget about the socks.

I tiptoed toward the bathroom and ran a stream of water on my head. The water pinched, it was so cold. I ran a towel across my hair and face so fast that the joints of my arms twisted in pain. I grabbed some oil and rubbed it on my face and hair. I picked up a comb and ran it through my hair.

I was already late. I had less than one minute to get to the bus stop and board a bus so I could get to an interview. I did not have a job, so I had placed all my hopes on the interview, which was to take place fifteen kilometers from my house. I had eagerly waited for this day and did not sleep the night before. I kept tossing and turning on the bed, thinking about how my life would changed if I got the job. I could buy a car, build a palace, save a lot. I was building castles in the air. And I hated myself for counting my chickens before they hatched.

I had to make up the time, because I had been waiting for this day. I had been as patient as a farmer waiting for the harvesting season. But time seemed to move faster. Seconds seemed like minutes.

I looked in the mirror and was disappointed at what I saw. It was a stranger; it was not me. I smiled to remove the creases on my face, but I looked more miserable. I did not brush my teeth. I prayed that God would take care of me.

I picked up my certificates and made my way to the door. My eyes happened to glance at the calendar. The tenth of October was supposed to be a Friday. Today was Thursday. I stepped back and looked more clearly. It was the ninth of October. What a fool I had made of myself. My eyes remained glued to the calendar as if it had dropped down from the sky. I felt like screaming with laughter, but my body was so tired, I sat down and rested. I realized I had one more chance to try my luck.

Assignment 16
With your classmates, identify the mistakes in the original version of this composition.

Assignment 17
Write an essay that illustrates the saying "better late than never."

Chapter 2

Fluency

Fluency incorporates the usage of the following to make the story flow smoothly:

- the correct word(s)
- a logical pattern of ideas
- good transitions within and between paragraphs

Let us discuss the first two in this chapter and the last one in Volume two of this book.

Correct Words

As discussed in chapter 1, in composition writing we use sentences—with the correct spelling, punctuation, and grammar—to communicate what we want to say. Words are useful labels for objects we know about or see around us, but their full meaning is revealed only when they are placed within the framework of a sentence—the basic human unit of expression. Through written sentences, we make our thoughts known to the reader. The most important person in the communication of ideas is the reader. He cannot read your mind if the words are not arranged in a clear enough manner to convey a message.

Logical Pattern of Ideas

A sentence is a group of words organized in a sensible manner to express a thought.

Sample Sentences

Clear: My father is a headmaster.
Unclear: In the case of my father he works as the head of all the teachers in that school.

Basic Sentence Pattern: Word Order

Before we discuss this important topic, we must recall our grammar lessons, and familiarize ourselves with the parts of speech:

1. Noun: the name of a person, place, or thing, e.g., Joseph, woman, Nairobi, cat, bus, etc.
2. Verb: a doing word, e.g., to run, to fight, to sing, to slap
3. Pronoun: a word used in a place of a noun, e.g., I, she, me, you, them, it, etc.
4. Adjective: describes a noun, e.g., bad, good, sharp, better, etc.
5. Adverb: describes a verb, e.g., happily, quietly, hurriedly

6. Preposition: a word used with a noun or pronoun to make phrases, e.g. on, with, over, into, in, etc.

Make sure you understand the parts of speech before proceeding; proper sentence construction depends on them. A sentence usually consists of a subject and a verb. The subject is the focus of the action, i.e., the verb.

Assignment 18
Make a list of all the parts of speech.

Sample Sentences

- Mr. Khaemba teaches.

This is a grammatically correct sentence. The subject is Mr. Khaemba and the verb is the action he does, i.e., teaching.

- Mr. Khaemba teaches English.

A sentence may contain an object, i.e., the thing (usually a noun) to which the action is directed. In this sentence, *Mr. Khaemba* is the subject, *teaches* is the verb, and *Kiswahili* is the object.

Every sentence must begin with a capital letter and end with a full stop (or period). By substituting different words, we can create many sentences

Subject	Verb	Objects
Brian	writes	stories.
They	read	books.
Malaysia	teaches	furniture.

Not all combination are possible. This is because grammatical rules must be obeyed. For instance, it would be wrong to say "they makes furniture" because "s" is not added to a verb when the sentence begins with a plural noun or pronoun. Sentences must make sense. It does not make any sense to say, for example, "Brian makes science." Instead, say "Brian is a scientist" or "Brian studies science."

Assignment 19
Draw a table similar to the one below. Write various subjects, verbs, and objects in the appropriate columns.

Subject	Verb	Object

Assignment 20
Using the subjects, verbs, and objects in your completed table to create ten sentences that makes sense.

Adjectives and Adjectival Phrases
Expand a sentence by adding an adjectival phrase. Take, for example, the sentence *Khaemba makes shoes*. This sentence is grammatically correct, but we do not know what kind of shoes he makes. To encourage people to keep reading your composition, describe things more deeply. It is like cooking meat; you can eat boiled meat. But to make it taste good, you have to add salt, pepper, and other seasonings.

Let us consider some ways in which the basic sentence structures can be expanded with adjectives. For example, in the sentence *Mrs Gray makes shoes*, we can add an adjective to the object to show what kind of shoes: *Mrs Gray makes <u>leather</u> shoes*.

Remember that adjectives describe nouns—in terms of size, age, color, origin, material, and quality/type. A number of adjectives used together creates an adjectival phrase.

Quantity	Quality/Type	Color	Origin	Material	Noun
One	beautiful	black	American	leather	bag.
Five	new	white	Chinese	clay	pots.
Two	young	brown	Swahili		boys.
An	energetic	black			lady.
Three	tall and fat	black			men.
One	big	brown	German		car.

Write:
A beautiful, large, black, American leather bag …
Five new, white, Chinese clay pots …
A young, brown Mexican boy …
An energetic, old, black lady …
The tall, fat, black man …

Do not write:
A large, beautiful, American, black leather bag …

Five white, new, Chinese clay pots …
An energetic, black, old lady …

You can add more than one adjective to a sentence. However, avoid adjectival phrases that are too long; for instance, rather than writing "a good, young, ten-year-old American girl," Write "the young American girl who is ten years old is a good person. "Keep is simple and short.

Assignment 21
Make a table of adjectival phrases following the above pattern. Then write ten sentences containing those adjectival phrases.

Sample Essay: "A Pleasant Surprise"

My sister and I went to the market early in the morning; then we made our way home. When we arrived, each of us carrying a big white bag, we found everybody looking happy. My father was in his usual, smart, blue cotton suit and a pair of new, black leather shoes. As the saying goes, every cloud has a silver lining.

On our way home, we'd seen someone selling raffle tickets. My clever, young sister asked me, "Why can't I play this game?"

"Oh, you can," I told her. I put my hand into my pocket and fished out my beautiful, small, brown leather wallet. I opened it and gave her money to buy the ticket. I filled out her name and address on the ticket and gave it back.

Suddenly, there was a commotion. People were running toward one area, shouting "thief! thief!" We forgot about the raffle ticket and rushed to see what the matter was. People had surrounded a huge, dirty, black man. Everyone was throwing stones at him. The man fell on the ground, blood oozing from his nose and mouth like water rushing down a mountain.

It was not a pleasant sight, so we went home. "What is that?" asked my sister, pointing at a small red booth. "It is a place where people make calls." I said. "What is it called?" she asked. I told her it was called a telephone box.

We took our time getting home. Everyone was as happy as a king. My sister asked my mother why. "It is you, my girl," my mother said. "You are famous!"

"Why, Mummy?" my sister asked.

My mother put down the blue plastic bucket she was carrying and asked, "What did you do on the way home? Did you play the lottery?" Then she paused and was quiet for so long you would have thought she was Isaac Newton formulating the law of gravity.

"You won!" she said finally. "It was announced on television a few minutes ago. Where is the money?"

My mind was in turmoil; I did not know exactly how to answer her. Each time, I tried to open my mouth, the saliva disappeared, and my mouth turned as dry as a desert. I gazed at the green wooden door that led into the main house. Then I remembered; because of the confusion caused by the thief, we had not waited for the for results to be announced.

"What went wrong?" Dad asked. "Didn't they give you the money?"

"We didn't wait," I replied.

Comments

The composition shows the use of adjectival phrases. However, students are not expected to use as many adjectival phrases as are included above. This was meant only for practice. In your compositions, try to use at least five adjectival phrases.

Assignment 22

Use adjectival phrases to write an essay about your first day in primary school.

Assignment 23

Construct ten sentences with adverbs. Remember your sentences should show when or how the action took place.

Assignment 24

Make a table with five columns headed subject, adverb, adjectives, and noun in that order. Then form sentences using each type of word.

Subject	Adverb	Verb	Adjective	Noun

Here is a list of some commonly used adverbs:

* usually

Tony is usually a happy boy.

* often

It often rains in April.

* occasionally

They occasionally visit their rural home.

- nearly

The milk nearly boiled over.

- recently

I recently heard that Mr Wafula teaches at Hilltop Academy School.

- soon

Part 2 of the play will be staged soon after part 1.

- scarcely

They scarcely had enough to eat.

- certainly

We certainly cannot do without money.

- suddenly

After drinking illegal liquor, they suddenly fell sick.

Building Paragraphs

There comes a time when the idea to be expressed is too long to be expressed as one sentence. You have to put several sentences together to express one or more ideas. This is called a paragraph. Note: a group of sentences with more than one idea is not a paragraph. A paragraph should deal with single idea. For example:

> Established four years ago, Eldorock Elementary School is located in a small slum, west of Kasumi. Sweet melodies of birds have found homes in the fences that surround the compound. The students are proud of this school, which is headed by Mr. Morgan Doe.

This paragraph tells us

- the name of the school
- the location of the school
- when it was started
- about the surroundings
- who heads the school
- the attitude of the pupils toward the schools

The first paragraph of a composition should not only convey a single idea but also encourage the reader to continue with the rest of the composition. Consider this: if visitors find your sitting room dirty, they will assume that the bedroom and toilet are dirty too. They will think that you are dirty people and may dislike you immediately. This is also the case in composition writing. First paragraphs should thrill. Create a good impression by using a topic sentence, a supporting sentence, and a conclusion, the last sentence.

The Topic Sentence

The main idea in a paragraph is expressed in a topic sentence, usually the first sentence. It serves as an introduction to the content of the paragraph. It should also be captivating and encourage people to keep reading your work. For example, in this paragraph, the first sentence is the topic sentence:

> It was eight o'clock, but there were no teachers at school. The pupils were silent as they waited for the lessons to start. Gong! That was the bell signaling the pupils to go to assembly. The pupils marched slowly toward the assembly, like sheep without a shepherd.

The topic sentence prepares us for the rest of the story. We wonder what could have happened to the teachers and want to read to find out.

Assignment 25

Construct a captivating topic sentence.

Supporting Sentences

These are the sentences that follow the topic sentence. They explain or provide more information about the topic introduced by the first sentence. Each supporting sentence gives more details about the main idea. Supporting sentences are like fundraisers who also give money to support the project. In this case, the project is the topic sentence. For example:

> Every day, I hear over the radio that people have lost their lives in road accidents [topic sentence]. In most cases, the accident are caused by drivers who choose to drive while they are drunk. But I also learned that some of these drivers had not gone to the driving school. Many are *matatu* (minibus) drivers who are out to make some quick money [supporting sentences].

This paragraph has unity. All of the sentences focus on road accidents. The writer has concentrated on one idea.

Assignment 26

Starting with the topic sentence provided below, construct seven supporting sentence to complete the paragraph: Nowadays, everyone is talking about AIDS …

The Last Sentence

The final sentence in each paragraph should
- create enough suspense to make the reader desire to know more
- prepare for the topic sentence in the next paragraph

For example:

> ………………………………………John Doe sat on the floor. He looked squarely at the policeman. Blood oozed from his left ear. His hands were tied behind his back, and his legs were chained to a pole. The wall behind was smeared

with his blood. The policeman paced up and down the room with a whip. He had promised to make John Doe into crocodile food if he did not reveal where the bottle of mercury was. But who could have taken the mercury from the safe last night?

The concluding paragraph should be interesting, amusing, include a proverb relevant to the subject matter, or ask a question worth thinking about.

Assignment 27
Refer to the above essay concluding paragraph and Construct three captivating concluding paragraphs of your choice for any topic you choose.

Comments
Paragraphs are organized in chronological order, that is, the order in which the events took place. Remember to stick to the topic throughout the story. Each paragraph should be short and to the point; it should have eight to ten sentences. Long paragraphs, particularly those with long words and long sentences, make the reader reread the paragraph over and over in an attempt to discover what you were trying to say.

Assignment 28
Create paragraphs of about eight to ten sentences each on the following topics.
- a fire
- a school
- an encounter with a lion

Paragraph Organization
A composition should have at least three main paragraphs, namely
- introduction;
- body; and
- Conclusion.

The body should be several paragraphs long, and the introduction and conclusion should be at least one paragraph each. If one were writing about drug abuse, for example, he or she might organize his paragraphs as follows:

- Paragraph 1: the meaning of the term "drug abuse"
- Paragraph 2: caused by bad company
- Paragraph 3: caused by desire to run away from problems
- Paragraph 4: as a result, drugs become a habit
- Paragraph 5: effects of drugs on the body
- Paragraph 6: help for the addicted person
- Paragraph 7: ways to avoid the problem

Assignment 29
Write an essay about drug abuse using the points given above.

Beginning a New Paragraph

A new paragraph starts when there is a change in topic or time, or there are similar people, actions, or topics.

- Change in the topic: If in the first paragraph you describe a school compound, the second paragraph should describe the classroom. If you describe a farmer named Mr. Mark Smith, in the next paragraph describe Mrs. Eunice Juma, his farm manager.
- Change in time: This can be in future or the past. The paragraph may start in one of the following ways: *A few days later ... A moment ago ... The next day ... Not long afterward*, etc.
- Similar topics: If you want to compare one topic to another topic—e.g., compare your school to your brother's school—start the second paragraph in any of a number of ways, including: *Like my school, my brother's school ... The same thing applies to ... In the same way*, etc.

Assignment 30

The sentences below represent the beginning of a story. Read them carefully and then complete the story. Apply the techniques you have learned about paragraph construction, and write at least twelve paragraphs.

I had walked in the darkness for a long time. Just when I started to wonder where I was, I saw a light in the distance ...

Chapter 3

Writing a Captivating Composition

Descriptions and Explanations

Usually, the examiner will look for interesting stories. To achieve this, you can use similes, idioms, proverbs, and metaphors. They enrich your language. A dull composition will make examiners lose interest, which may make them give you a low grade.

Sample Essay: "A Rainy Day"

It was raining. My brothers, mother, and sisters were in the house. We were drinking tea with milk. It continued raining, and a lot of water was running down the slope. The water falling on the iron roof made a lot of noise, and one could not hear another person drinking tea. The tea was so hot, my youngest brother was unable to drink it. We continued drinking tea, and the rain continued raining. At one point our roof started leaking, because the rain was heavy. My mother moved the utensils to one corner. Yesterday it had rained heavily too, and it could rain tomorrow. It has been raining throughout the month, and there were several frogs in the stagnant water around our house. They made a lot of noise every night. The farmers thought the rain was good, but too much rain meant they had to plow their farms. The cows, sheep, goats, camel, and donkey were happy, because now there was plenty of grass. The rooster also entered the house to get shelter. The chicks and hen had come earlier, before it started to rain. It seemed that it would rain for the whole afternoon and even the night. These days, the rain has become too much. When we finished tea, everybody went to sleep as it continued to rain. We also ate supper.

Is the above composition interesting? Is it well organized? What about the language? The truth is the composition is poorly organized.

You can make your composition captivating and interesting by
- treating the reader to a moment of suspense, that is, making them want to find out what will happen next
- creating an unexpected event, for instance:

(a) A swarm of bees disturbs people counting money at a *harambee* (fundraising) meeting.

(b) A masked stranger steals from a woman; when the mask is removed, the thief is revealed to be the woman's son.

(c) You expect visitors; you cook a lot of food, but they don't come at the expected time. You share the food with your neighbors. Then your guests arrive.

(d) After taking the Kenya Certificate of Primary Education (KCPE), you receive an offer letter from a good national school. It was pomp and circumstance all night as you celebrated the good news. A closer look the following day reveals that the results were not yours but those of your namesake.

Sample Essay: Robbery at Daylight

On Sunday morning, I woke up at the crack of dawn. I had a lot of homework to do, so I did not go to the church. I went to the bathroom and took a cold shower; as the saying goes, cleanliness is next to godliness. I had barely settled down to do my homework when I heard a knock at the door. I thought it was my father returning home from his nightshift, but when I opened the door I was surprised to see two complete strangers standing there.

One was tall and thin with a round face, and the other one was short and plump, like an oil drum. The tall man looked sickly; the skin was stretched tightly over his bony face. His eyes were deep set, and his eyelids were so thin, I thought they would not be able to close and open.

As he gave me his hand to say hello, I felt like I was holding the hand of some dark figure from my dreams. He looked very old; from the way he gripped my hand, I thought he might be more than fifty. I automatically respected him; as the saying goes, old is gold. The short man was charming. He looked young; his eyes seemed to smile, and his voice rose and fell like a singing bird. He was attractive; his clothes looked formal, I said hello to him with smile. Our family did not usually welcome strangers to the house, but I did not want to assume that they were bad or good, as I am a strong believer in the English saying "don't judge a book by its cover."

Something about them made me invite them into the house. They sat facing each other, and I sat between them. I told them to make themselves at home and went to the kitchen to prepare some tea. The old man said something I did not understand, and I saw the short man dip his hand into his pocket and fish out a hundred shilling note.

"Would you go and buy my father something to eat?" he asked. "Anything." I was no hurry to ask them why they had come, as such behavior would be uncultured. As the saying goes, "hurry, hurry has no blessing."

"I will buy a loaf" I replied.

"Just something to put in his stomach," the short man said. "He is very hungry." I went out of the house, shutting the door behind me. I took off for the shop as fast as lightning. I had one worry at the back of my mind. I heard a wild voice telling me not to go. *But the old man is desperate; he has not eaten*, another voice protested.

I arrived at the shop and bought the food, but on my way back. I met an old woman. Her skin was flabby and hair was uncombed. She pleaded with me. "My boy, please show me the way to the …"

I felt like pushing her out of my way, so I could run away from her and back to the strangers in the house. But her eyes filled with tears. She seemed to have no place to sleep. I felt sorry for her, so I responded to her question quickly. But she said, "I cannot understand."

"Oh God," I muttered. "I have to show her." I took her by the arm and walked as slowly as she did. Due to her age, the pace was as slow as a snail's. I tried to walk fast, but there was no point. Finally, I decided to run away from her. I returned to my house. As I opened the door, I knew something was wrong. The room was completely empty.

Comments

The writer of the composition above attracted the examiner's interest when he welcomed the strangers into the house. The story took a turn when he returned from the shop to find that the strangers had stolen everything in the sitting room. The essay ends there; we don't know if he was ever able to find the furniture. This is suspense.

Assignment 31

Using the techniques you have learned and the outline below, write an essay titled "Wedding Day." Describe a series of events, and let the story take a different turn each time.

Outline

- beautiful bride
- handsome bridegroom
- arrived in a convoy of vehicles
- everyone in a jovial mood
- Church packed to capacity.
- pastor conducts wedding ceremony
- pastor asks for reasons why the two cannot be wed
- congregation falls silent; you could have heard a pin drop
- bride looks uneasy
- bridegroom feels hollow
- people exchange telling glances
- "That is my man! That is my man!" shouts the bride

- she fights with the groom's long-time lover, who beats up the bride
- the lover and bridegroom go out of the church, holding hands together
- bees emerge and start stinging people, who run in different directions

Assignment 32
Following the guidelines given above, write an interesting essay titled "Adventure in the Forest." Use composition flavor, similes, proverbs, etc.

Chapter 4

Speechwriting

A speech is a talk or address given in public. It is organized in the same way as a composition. However, a speech is different, because the speaker begins by addressing the audience. For example, a headmaster might begin his speech with the following: "Honorable members of staff, students, and parents, we have come to the end of this long term."

When you are writing down a speech, incorporate the actual words used by the speaker. Opening and closing quote marks are used to enclose those words. Closing quote marks are placed after the period or comma. For example: "I wish you a safe journey back home."

Speeches are written in present tense and identify the audience at the beginning, starting with the person who is regarded in the highest esteem or holds the highest post. For example: "Our guest of honor, education officers and teachers, parents, girls, and boys."

Assignment 33

Write speech that ends with the following words: "Let me take this opportunity to wish all of you a Merry Christmas and a truly prosperous New Year. Thank you." Any occasion might be appropriate for this ending; for instance, a speech given by the president during the Independence Day celebrations. Note that each new paragraph has opening quote marks, but only the final paragraph has closing quote marks.

Sample Speech: independence Day
"Fellow Countrymen, ladies and gentlemen, we assemble here today to observe the thirty-sixth anniversary of the day we severed our links with colonization and assumed full responsibility for the shaping our own destiny. We waged war to win our freedom. It is always tempting on Jamuhuri Day to talk about our late president and those who shed their blood for this nation. We praise them because their struggle made us what we are.

"But today as we celebrate Jamuhuri Day, I want to discuss my dream for Kenya. My vision for the future is to see that all youths are employed and that unemployment becomes something in the past. I want to see a nation where basic education is free and compulsory for its citizens. I have a dream that one day this nation will rise above the tribal line. The Luhya, the Kikuyus, the Luo, and many others tribes will all unite and form a single tribe and speak a single language.

"Ladies and gentlemen, it is my wish that any national holiday falling on a day of worship is celebrated the following day. I will make it possible for people to attend the national holiday celebrations without disrupting their religious routines.

"I have today released more than ten thousand prisoners to join their families, friends, and relatives during the Christmas holiday. I hope they will become law-abiding citizens of this country.

Finally fellow Kenyans, ladies and gentlemen, I urge you to maintain peace and unity. As you all know, united we stand, divided we fall. Let me take this opportunity to wish all of you a Merry Christmas and a truly prosperous New Year. Thank you."

Comments
This speech uses the pronouns *I* and *we*.

Assignment 34
Write a speech given by a headmaster during a parents' day. Here are some guidelines to follow:
- Recount some of the outstanding things the class has done in the past.
- Congratulate the pupils.
- Thank the parents for their cooperation.
- Thank the guest of honor for finding time to attend the ceremony.

Assignment 35
You are the guest of honor during a prize-giving day at a school. Write the speech you would give.

Assignment 36
You are the chief of your village, and a war has broken out. Prepare the speech you would give to the warriors just before they set out for battle.

Assignment 37
You are the headmaster of a secondary school. Write a speech welcoming the form 1 students at your school.

Chapter 5

Letter Writing

Assignment 38a

Write a friendly letter to a friend who was transferred to another a school; tell her how you have been. Inquire about her well being. Tell her how you have been. Give her some news about your school and your family. Ask when you will be able to see her. Send greetings and best wishes.

Letter Format

Remember to follow the appropriate format for a friendly letter.

Write your address here
Write the date here

Write the salutation here, e.g., **Dear ...**
Write the body of the letter in one or more paragraphs.
Write the valediction (complimentary close), e.g., **Yours sincerely**
Write your name

Here is a complete letter:

Baltimore Academy,
P.O Box 52,
Sacramento.
May 06, 2015

Dear Rebecca,

Hello, and how have you been? We are fine and keeping busy. I hope you are well too.

You might be interested to know that this term I was number one in our class. I hope to work harder and maintain that position!

My parents keep telling me that they miss you, since you used to visit us almost every day. They always tell me that you have a good character. This makes me want to be like you. Perhaps my grades improved this term because I arranged for private tutoring, like you told me to do.

Please write, and tell me when we can next meet. I would be glad if you stayed with use during the forthcoming holiday, at least for a few days.

I am sending hearty greetings from Mum, Dad and everyone else here at home and at school. Give my regards to your parents and friends.

Yours Sincerely,

Irene Stella

Assignment 38b
Read the following five sentences carefully, and write other five points that Rebecca might use to reply the above letter.

- It was really nice to hear from you.
- I was glad to learn that you did well in class.
- How is my former teacher, Mr. Justus?
- I send warm greetings from our family.
- School closes on April 4, and I shall arrange a visit to your home

Assignment 39a
Write a friendly letter to your father; imagine that he works far from your home.

Assignment 39b
Write a letter to your headmaster apologizing for being absent from school without permission. This will be an official letter. The layout (format) of an official letter is different from that of a friendly letter. It should have both your address and that of the person to whom you are writing.

Write your address here.
Write the date here.

Write the name of the other person here.
Write the address of the other person here.

Re: add the topic here.

Include the salutation, e.g., **Dear Sir/Madam,**

Introduce yourself and give the reason you are writing. Explain what you plan to do in the future to fix the situation, if applicable.

Include the valediction, e.g., **Yours sincerely,**

Add your signature.

Write your name here.

For example:

James Martin
PO Box 195
Port Mombasa
March 27, 2015

The Headmaster,
Examination Elementary School,
P.O Box 52
Turbo

Re: Apology for absence from school

Dear Sir,
I am James Martin, one of the top pupils in standard 8. I would like to apologize for leaving school without permission yesterday.

My absence was caused by a problem at home. My mother was sick, and my father had to rush her to the hospital. Hence, I had to remain at home to look after my younger brother. Fortunately, my mother was treated and discharged, and I was able to come to school today.

I realize that I should have informed the office that I would be away in advance. I promise not to repeat the mistake in future.

Yours sincerely,

[signature]
James Martin
Standard 8

Assignment 40
Compare and contrast the two types of letters, and write down the differences between them. Make a table like the one below.

Friendly Letter	Official Letter
Has one address	Has two addresses

Assignment 41
Write an official letter to a headmaster seeking admission to a secondary school.

Chapter 6

Accuracy

Accuracy is the ability to use the following:
- correct verbs
- correct tenses
- appropriate punctuation
- appropriate vocabulary
- correct spelling

Language usage is what makes a composition good or bad. In the national exams, marks given to compositions range from 0 to 40. To earn high marks for an essay, a student must display a mastery of the English language and writing standards. To make this point clear, we shall look at compositions in four categories.

Category 1 (1–10 marks)

> My father does not love smoking uncle come our home smoke sitting chairs. When father waked up not happy. But since his uncle is brothers did not say any thing

This is the lowest category of composition. However, there are students who write worse compositions than this. Some students cannot write at all. This composition displays very poor mastery of English, and it is of a low standard. It is full of grammatical errors; for example:

- *my father do not* instead of *my father does not*
- *he waked up* instead of *he woke up*

Read more storybooks and speak and write in English more often at school and home to avoid this situation.

Category 2 (11–20 marks)

> My father, who does not like smoking, was quite unhappy when we woke up and found Uncle smoking in our sitting room. My uncle had come to pay us a visit. He sat on the sofa, smoking and looking very happy as a king.

Usually, my dad would ask visitors to smoke outside the house, but he found it rather hard to ask the same of his brother.

This category represents compositions by average students. This pupil gives a clear account of events; the story has a good flow and is fairly interesting. However, the language is plain; there are no proverbs, idioms, or similes, etc. The pupil could improve his essay with practice; he could read more storybooks outside class. Look at his sentence construction: "very happy as a king" should be "as happy as a king." Pupils should be careful not to use similes and other expressions that they have not learned in class.

Category 3 (21–30 marks)

He was irritated. He had always hated smoking and now he had woken up in a stuffy sitting room. Anger was written all over my father's face as he faced my uncle, who sat comfortably, looking as happy as a king.

My uncle, whose teeth and figure spoke volumes about his smoking, had lit up right in the room; the aggressive fumes of smoke would have put a chimney to shame. My father usually preferred people to smoke outside, but with his elder brother, he tried to restrain himself, giving credence to the old adage "blood is thicker than water."

This particular composition would earn high marks. It is free of grammatical errors. The vocabulary is varied. The story is interesting. This is what is expected in composition writing. To attain this level of writing, one needs to be a good reader of storybooks, novels, magazines, and newspapers.

Category 4 (31–40 marks)

My father, who abhors smoking, was visibly offended. When he woke up, he found a stuffy, smoke-filled living room, much to his disgust. Dumbfounded, his eyes moved from his brother's soot-black teeth to his nicotine-stained fingers, which told volumes about my uncle's lifelong addiction to smoking. Like a zombie, my visiting uncle had planted himself on our sofa, mindlessly emitting thick, offensive fumes. Usually, Dad would not stomach such obnoxious behavior in the house; without mincing words, he would promptly give the culprit a piece of his mind. But with his elder brother, he found his hands tied behind his back. He let my uncle go Scot-free. Blood is thicker than water.

This composition would have earned top marks. (The goal of this book is to help you write similar compositions.) The writer has a strong command of the language and the subject matter. The vocabulary choices are good; no hard words are used. The reader's interest is sustained throughout. The story is captivating. The writer is imaginative, likely due to wide reading outside of class. The work is outstanding and would appeal to examiners. You too can do this if you work hard.

The writer of the composition below tried to employ good writing techniques.

Sample Essay: "Bomb Blast"

A bomb is made of components that explode, causing large-scale destruction of buildings and lives. Human beings turn bombs into weapons of mass destruction. When a bomb explodes, it causes a loud bang, and the property and people around the square where it has exploded rarely escape unhurt. Bombs are lethal weapons.

Bomb blasts are frequently reported in the Middle East countries. These countries are always at loggerheads. Bomb explosions are seldom experienced in African countries like Kenya, Uganda, and Tanzania. Kenyans got a rude shock when they turned on their radios on in August 1998 and heard the broadcaster announce that Kenya was under attack!

A mysterious object had hit the center of the capital city, Nairobi, bringing down the giant "Ufundi" Plaza Building and reducing the America embassy to rubble! A similar explosion occurred in Tanzania at almost the same time, claiming a lot of lives.

Chills ran down my body. I was perplexed and stunned. I ran to the nearest phone box and dialed the number of a school friend who stayed in Nairobi.

"Kelly, are you okay?" I asked immediately, without using a greeting. He assured me of his safety. Then I demanded the latest news.

He told me that the day had begun like any other bright day. Nairobi, as usual, woke up, and people streamed into the streets to struggle and take home their daily bread. At ten o'clock the twin bomb blasts exploded in Nairobi and Dar es Salaam. "As I am speaking, a huge pile of concrete, which was once "Ufundi" plaza House, is lying on people! "Ufundi" Plaza House is destroyed."

I almost jumped out of my skin. "Oh God! Why Kenya of all the countries?" I muttered to myself.

Kenyan government officials were heroes. The minister of international cooperation was on the air promptly, assuring Kenya that the security forces were alert, and everything was under control. The Israeli army flew in and helped to remove the bodies trapped in the debris. They fought a brave war and saved some lives. The rescue team worked under Major Agrey of the Navy. Good Samaritans were asked to donate blood to the casualties. Kenyans responded to the call and donated blood wholeheartedly. As the saying goes, a friend in need is a friend indeed. At the end of day one, about four victims of the blast were thought to be still trapped under the debris. Under the direction of the brave and devoted Israeli Army, the rescuers continued to look for survivors using hoes, hooks, and their bare hands under the glare of the spotlights.

Meanwhile the survivors, including the American ambassador to Kenya, described their ordeal to the international press amid tears. The American ambassador had been caught by the blast just as she was leaving a meeting with a Kenyan government official. Time and again, the television showed the American president warning the culprits to give themselves up. He promised not to leave any stone unturned to ensure that international terrorism was destroyed. And for sure he lived up to his promise. One by one, the terrorists were caught, and justice was done

Comments

The above composition is a dry one. To some extent, the writer can be excused, because the topic does not allow him to add flavor, and forcing certain words into a composition is not allowed. Pupils are advised not to force words into compositions or use words they do not understand. In the following essay, the writer used more exciting words.

Sample Essay: "The Day I Will Never Forget"
The morning still lingers in my memory. It was a cold morning with a chilly breeze. I had woken up rather later than usual. Some voice kept whispering to me, "This is your day." But I quickly brushed away that idea, although I had come to believe that I had a sixth sense that could tell me whenever something unusual was going to happen.

I jumped out of bed, took a warm shower, and put on my best shoes, which my younger sister had helped me select. I grabbed my schoolbag, threw in a few books, and rushed to school. The teacher on duty had a deaf ear about lateness, so I increased my pace.

I had walked for barely ten minutes when I saw a brown object lying on the ground, a stone's throw away. I was curious to find out what on earth it could be. I moved like a cat pouncing on a rat; when I got close I was disappointed to find it was a piece of wood. I got worked up and gave the wood a hard kick. Underneath it was a purse.

I could not believe my eyes. I thought my imagination was playing tricks on me, that it was a trap and someone was hiding and watching me, so I turned around. There were no signs of human beings in the vicinity. In fact, the place was as silent as a grave.

By then, I was trembling from head to toe, like a hen dropped into cold water. My mouth was wide open; one might think I could see better using my mouth than using my eyes. My eyes were glued to the purse as if it had been dropped from heaven. My body lost strength, and my schoolbag fell down—plop. My whole body shuddered as I hesitantly bent down to pick the purse. I pocketed it and made a U-turn back home. I ran as fast as my thin legs could carry me, occasionally stopping and turning behind to ensure nobody was following me.

As I approached our homestead, I gradually slowed down. I crept through the hedge and through the backdoor and made my way to my bedroom. I securely locked my bedroom and plucked courage to open the wallet. I searched the contents of the purse.

It was filled with piles of new bank notes. I knew my day had finally come. As the saying goes, every dog has its day.

"Hauu-uu-ui!" I screamed when I realized each bill was a thousand-shilling note. A mixture of joy and excitement filled my heart. I counted the money; it was one hundred thousand shillings. I paced around my tiny bedroom building castles in the air, thinking about how I would spent my sudden windfall.

I thought about whether to tell my father or my mother first. This news would be pleasant music to their ears. I decided to gather them together and then break the news to both of them at once.

Suddenly the door flew wide open! Two strangers almost knocked me down. They pointed pistols of at me and ordered me to surrender!

Comments

The above essay has captivating words, so it will earn high marks. Another way of sustaining the reader's interesting is with dialogue.

Sample Essay: "A Narrow Escape"
"Let me rest," Tony said.

"Sure, we can have a rest," said Frank. "That was a narrow escape. How did you manage to go though the cypress fence with the dogs hot on your heels?"

"It was easy," replied Tony. "A hard kick on the mouth of one dog was enough to make all of them scamper for their safety. How did you manage to escape? I thought I'd left you up a tree!"

"Yes, but the farmer and the dogs were concentrating more on you," Frank said. "So I jumped down from the tree and escaped through the main gate."

"You must be brighter than I am," said Tony. "Any mangoes in your pocket?"

"None," answered Frank.

"Look!" Tony said. "I managed to escape with all these mangoes, despite the chase from the dogs and the farmer, so who is the clever one?"

Comments

Dialogue is another way of giving the examiner information he needs to know. Be sure to use the correct punctuation and break your paragraphs in the appropriate places. (Look at the format used in the above essay.) Following are basic guidelines for using dialogue.

- Use quotation marks to show that you are quoting the exact, spoken words, for example, *"I want to pass my exams," Joel said.* Start each line of dialogue with a capital letter.
- Whenever the speaker changes, begin a new paragraph. However, dialogue should not dominate the whole composition or Essay

Assignment 41

Using the techniques described above, write a conversation between a teacher and his Student, Mary Doe, who is the class representative. The teacher wants to know why the classroom is dirty. Mary gave the teacher the below explanation as the reason why the class is dirty:

Sample Essay: "All that Glitters Is Not Gold"
".....................I woke up at crack of morning I take tea leave milk, I ware my uniform of school and washed my face and I rushed to school. When I reach at the gate I see money on the ground. I this I a delighted to late to school.

I picked it with a smile and ran to school very faster faster. I told my friend about the Mani I buy those sweets and we eat at break time. and that why class is dirtly sir."

Comments

This essay has several mistakes, including incorrect verb tenses, word usage, spelling grammar, and punctuation and even the topic is wrong. It's to long and not to the point. Correct the above essay. Rewrite it in the perfect form.

Assignment 43

Rewrite the essay above, using the correct verb tenses, grammar, spelling, punctuation, and words. Insert proverbs, idioms, and similes as appropriate. Make it as interesting as you can.

Sample Essay
All the arrangements had been made. Invitations had been sent to the guests, and they all agreed to attend the wedding ceremony.

My cousin, who had a diploma in interior design, decorated the great hall carefully and nicely. Several types of food had been prepared. Even at our doorstep it was obvious that something pleasant was in the air. It was the beginning of a new life. The party was to be the climax of my wedding.

By midday, people from all walks of life—fat and thin, big and small, rich and poor—had entered our compound. They all were dressed to kill. Mini skirts, jeans ties, and jackets gave the compound a happy mood.

The night before I did not get a wink of sleep. I kept on tossing on my bed, curious about how the next day would look. But morning never seemed to come; as the saying goes, a watched pot never boils. I prayed for the success of the day. Then the morning arrived!

The beautiful rays of the sun hit the ground at a gentle angle. Soft, lovely music could be heard among the noise and cheers coming from the guests. I knew the day would be a success; as everyone knows, a good day is seen in the morning.

We set off with a convoy of eight cars to pick up the bride. Our driver reduced his speed gradually as we approached our destination. We had gone to the same secondary school. Both sets of parents had given the green light for us to marry each other. In fact. My future mother-in-law once said her daughter was lucky to bump into me. I was proud of that.

Finally we arrived. We honked for the gates to be opened. There was no response. The home looked like it had been deserted thousand of years ago! There was no trace of human life. The driver honked again and again. The sound went through the air like thunder, but still nobody appeared to open the gate.

"Matilda might have changed her mind," I whispered to myself. Smelling a rat, I jumped over the fence and made my way into the compound. When I looked inside the house, I did not like what I saw. A body lay sprawled on the ground. From where I stood, I could recognize the man. His clothes made my heart stop beating. They belonged to Matilda's father.

I felt worn out. I turned and made my way into the bedroom. I took the telephone receiver and pressed the number for the police. But before I could speak, I felt a cold touch at the back of my neck! It was ice cold. I turned abruptly.

The father of Matilda stood just inches away from me. Sorrow was written on his face. His eyes were swollen from what I thought was crying. He was trying to tell me something. I was looking at a ghost!

Finally, I heard him clearly: "She is dead," he said. It struck me like a stab in the heart. Tears rolled down my cheeks like a stream of water from a peak of a mountain. "It pains me to lose my daughter at such a tender age," lamented the old man.

This composition is captivating. Pupils are advised not to write dry compositions.

Chapter 7

Vocabulary

Below are lists of accurate vocabulary for various types of situations.

Expressing Anger
voice choked with anger, was irked, was enraged, his fury knew no bounds, speechless with fury, poured out his wrath on us, vented her anger on the poor children, quarreled angrily, hot-tempered, lost his temper, should have tamed his tongue, needs to keep her head/cool

Expressing Sadness
broken heart, choked with emotion, eyes red from weeping, she talked between sobs, eyes welled with tears, tears coursed down his cheeks, had a heavy heart, eyes were in flood of tears, sorrowful, wept uncontrollably, grief-stricken, needed a shoulder to cry on/sympathy and comfort

Expressing Fear
she felt fear grip her heart, his heart was pounding in his chest, blood froze in my veins, a chill ran down my spine, my blood ran cold, frightened, worried, tense, nervous, hair stood on end, paralyzed with horror, heart skipped a beat, I had the fright of my life, terrified and shaking like a leaf

Expressing Happiness
jumped in ecstasy, broke into a dance, radiant with joy, her eyes shone with delight, walked on air, felt on top of the world, feet scarcely touched the ground, full of enthusiasm, bubbling over with excitement, he was all smiles, her face brightened with delight, glittered like gold could not hide his joy, applauded thunderously, cheerful

Describing the Weather and Nature
hills hidden in the mist, a chilly morning, cloudless sky, sunny, scorching sun, sunlight filtered through holes in the roof, animals took shelter under the shady baobab trees, walked on the dusty road, birds chirped as they perched on a branch of an acacia tree, chattering of monkeys, by the sea shore, frogs croaked, the farmer heard goats bleat, cows moo and dogs bark, vast tract of forest, lush green grass, a strong wind blew, dark clouds gathered, the heavens opened, a storm broke, rain flooded the village, a heavy downpour, torrential floods raged, deafening thunder, lightning lit up the sky, rain cats and dogs, muddy roads, snow-capped mountains, valleys and hills, windy, calm weather, rainy season, his voice echoed in the forest, mouthwatering fruits, rustling of leaves

Showing Surprise

my heart leapt to my mouth, could not believe my eyes, dumbfounded/struck dumb, shocked beyond words, stood stock still in amazement, my heart was beating fast, I almost jumped out of my skin, profound shock and disbelief, he looked started, bewildered, in a dilemma

Describing Schools

quiet institution; workshop; library; well stocked with recommended books; dormitories; enough desks; founded on Christian traditions; highly qualified staff; role models; exemplary conduct; beyond reproach; school authorities/administration; sensitive to our needs; teacher-pupil rapport; boost morale; positive attitude toward learning; supportive parents; dedicated and eager-to-learn children; highly motivated; proud of her school; high discipline standards; attain good results in national examinations; impressive performance; extracurricular activities; excel in games; self-discipline and hard work encouraged; produced distinguished personalities—lawyers; doctors; teachers; academic giant; prize giving; best overall; lion's share of the trophies; school motto

Describing Life Situations

live from hand to mouth; eke out a living on the barren soil; meager earnings; shoulder the burden; take the bull by the horns; lend me a hand; he is an old hand; does it effortlessly; has the subject at her fingertips; join hands; put their heads together; exchange ideas; compare notes; wait with her fingers crossed; receive with open arms; makes a breakthrough; speaks eloquently; lets the cat out of the bag; enjoys the fruits of her labor; lines his own pockets; knows on which side his bread is buttered; goes the extra mile; where there is a will, there is a way; first come, first served; drags his feet; enormous task; work shoulder to shoulder; work diligently; punctual; determined; kill two birds with one stone; carry the day; keep the pot boiling; throw in the towel; charity begins at home

Describing a Person

strong, tall, and muscular; slim; emaciated; frail; short and thickset; bald; unkempt; clumsy; smartly dressed; neat; spick and span; teetotaler; respected; powerful; brilliant; humble man with a self-effacing nature; charming; focused; hardworking; honest; has a sense of honor; distinguished; supportive and understanding; well-groomed; eloquent speaker; articulate; confident; proud as a peacock; a wolf in sheep's clothing; jealous; she is slippery as a fish in water; do not judge a book by its cover; industrious; energetic; spotless; clean; thick in the head; outspoken; jack of all trades and master of none; as poor a church mouse

Describing a Relationship

engaged; apple of his eye; friendly; affectionately; walk hand in hand; head over heels in love; talk face to face; do not see eye to eye; it happened right under her nose; they did it behind his back; dance to his music; toe the line; the breadwinner in the family; the black sheep of the family; I put myself in his shoes; out of sight; out of mind; two heads are better than one; drive a wedge between friends; at logger heads with the teacher; gave the cold shoulder to; rub shoulders with; well wishers; live in harmony; peace, love, and unity; mindful of others welfare; pen pal; companion; in the same boat; I kept my distance; she rubbed her the wrong way; one and only; birds of a feather flock together

Describing Time

in a twinkling of an eye, time flew, a split-second action, promptly, urgent, not a minute to spare, work against time, work around the dock, eleventh hour, time stood still, spare time, leisure time, while away time, he is behind the times, she was born ahead of her time, I thought every minute would be my last, there is always a first time, the shadows were getting longer by the minute, dusk drew closer, in the sunset of his life

Describing a Road Accident

vehicle/*matatu*; speeding; overloaded; swerved; head-on collision/crash; oncoming; veered off the road; rolled and landed in a ditch; eyewitnesses; curious crowd gathered; stunned; sobbing uncontrollably; ghastly, horrifying scene; bodies trapped in the wreckage; lay in a pool of blood; I heard the screech of brakes; brakes failed; ambulance with siren blaring; tragic/fatal accident; died on the spot; sustained serious/minor injuries; rushed to hospital; admitted, treated, and discharged; escaped unhurt; traffic police; mangled wreck; towed away; hurry, hurry has no blessings; better late than never

Describing a Theft or Crime

thieves/thugs, armed with lethal weapons, broke into, ransacked the house, stole property, valued at, money in cash, beat up, raised the alarm, screamed for help, overcame the thugs, took to their heels, ran for dear life, chased, arrested, apprehended, handcuffed, police station, recorded statements, police cells, arraigned in court, suspect, charged with/accused of, found guilty/not guilty, sentenced to jail, strokes of the cane, fined, in mitigation, pleaded for mercy, first offender, judge ruled, such cases were on the increase, severe penalty, to deter would-be criminals, could not get away with it, held by police, helping the police with investigation, accomplice, abet, complicity, watchman, tied to a tree, the long arm of the law

Phrasal Verbs

Phrasal verbs can improve your compositions. Here are some examples:

- *break down*: fail to work, collapse
  The vehicle broke down and stalled halfway into the journey.
  The bereaved wife broke down during her husband's funeral.

- *break into*: enter by force, start doing something suddenly
  The burglars broke into the house and stole electronic equipment.
  They broke into a dance when they heard about the salary increase.

- *break out*: start suddenly
  A fierce fire broke out and reduced the house to ashes.

- *break up*: disperse
  The riot police broke up a crowd of demonstrators.

- *bring up*: raise a child
  Wafula had been brought up in Bungoma.

- *call for*: demand, require
  The education minister called on all teachers to avoid a showdown over the pay dispute.

- *call off*: postpone
  The meeting was called off at the eleventh hour.

- *call on/upon*: ask
  There were called upon to help stop the spread of HIV/AIDS.

- *carry away*: be excited
  He was carried away by the debate and could not hear you calling.

- *carry on*: continue
  Despite the criticism, Sue carried on with her work.

- *carry out*: do or execute
  Working mothers have to carry out many demanding duties.

- *check on*: verify
  The manager promised to check on the workers' complaints.

- *come about*: happen
  How did El Nino come about?

- *come across*: meet
  I had not come across a better woman than Isabella daughter.

- *deal with*: handle
  The government is dealing with the problem of corruption.

- *do without*: manage without
  One cannot do without food.

- *end in*: result in
  The quarrel ended in a fight.

- *end up*: conclude
  As a result of his stealing, he ended up in jail.

- *enter into*: venture, begin
  He entered politics at the age of twenty-two.

- *fade away*: die, end
  Old traditions are fading away.

- *fall apart*: break
  Their stormy marriage finally fell apart.

- *fall for*: be attracted to
  A day after we met, we fell for each other.

- *fall in*: collapse
  The roof fell in after it was weakened by termites.

- *fear for*: be concerned about
  I fear for their safety.

- *feel for*: sympathize
  Do people really feel for the street children?

- *figure out*: come to understand
  I could not figure out why the head of the department was blocking his promotion.

- *fill in*: complete (especially a form)
  Fill in the application carefully.

- *fit in*: mix smoothly
  The new pupil has fit in very well at St. Teresa's.

- *give in*: surrender
  The soldiers asked for reinforcements to make the enemy give in.

- *give out*: distribute
  The examination started soon after the invigilator gave out the test papers.

- *give up*: despair
  Do not give up after a first attempt; try again.

- *go after*: chase
  Members of public went after the child abductor and apprehended him.

- *go ahead*: continue
  Despite the rain, the football match went ahead.

- *go over*: check, revise
  It is better to go over your composition before handing it in.

- *go through*: suffer, struggle
  The Nairobi bomb blast victims and their relatives went through a lot of pain.

- *grow into*: become something
  Young Zipporah grew into a beautiful girl.

- gun down: kill
  The suspect was gunned down as he tried to flee.

- *hand in*: submit
  "Hand in your books for marking," the teacher said.

- *hand over*: transfer
  The outgoing district officer handed over the office to his replacement in a day-long ceremony.

- *order around*: keep on telling somebody what to do
  It is bad for children to order around the staff.

- *part with*: give away
  My father finds it hard to part with money.

- *point out*: direct attention toward
  The health officer pointed out the danger of eating uninspected meat.

- *put off*: postpone, discourage
  The drive to Nairobi has been put off until further notice.
  The speaker was put off by the shouting in the audience, and so she decided to sit down.

- *put out*: extinguish
  Put out the lamp before you fall asleep.

- *put up with*: tolerate
  She warned Kevin that she could not put up with his behavior.

- *rough up*: mishandle
  The suspect was roughed up by the police and frog-marched to the cells.

- *run into*: meet unexpectedly
  The truant boy ran into his teacher in town.

- *run out*: use up, suffer a shortage of
  The motorist ran out of petrol and needed to refuel.

- *set off*: start a journey
  We set off for Mombasa at dawn.

Sound and Motions

bang of a door
beat of a drum
blare of a trumpet
boom of a gun
bubbling of water
buzz of a telephone
chime of a clock
clatter of hooks
cracking of wood
crack of a whip
dripping of water
grinding of brakes
hissing of stream
hoot of a horn
jangling of chains
jingle of coins
lash of a whip
patter of feet
pealing of bells
report of a rifle
screeching of brake
slam of a door
stamping of feet
throb of a heartbeat
thunder of hoofs
tinkle of glass
toot of a horn
wail of a siren
zooming of an airplane

Assemblage
army of soldiers
band of musicians
board of directors
brood of pigeons
choir of singers
crew of sailors
flock of birds
flock of sheep
gang of thieves
herd of cattle
litter of pups
nest of birds
swarm of bees

pack of wolves
plague of locusts
pride of lions
team of players

Assemblage: Inanimate Objects
bale of cotton
bouquet of flowers
bunch of grapes
chest of drawers
crate of soda
fleet of ships
forest of trees
library of books
deck of cards
sheaf of corn
stack of hay
string of beads
tuft of grass

Colloquial Expressions
to blow one's trumpet: to boast
to burn the candle at both ends: overdo, work too much
to get into hot water: get into trouble
to give a cold shoulder: ignore
to have one's heart in one's mouth: be anxious
to hit below the belt: be unfair
to hit nail on the head: get something exactly right
to hold one's tongue: keep silent
to keep the pot boiling: keep on going
to make both ends meet: live within one's income
to make a clean breast of: confess
to pay a man in his own coin: treat a man as he has treated you
to put a cart before the horse: start at the wrong end
to sit on the fence: be neutral.
to smell a rat: be suspicious.
to sweep the board: take everything
to take French leave: remain absent without permission

Some Common Verbs with Suitable Adverbs

Verb	Adverb
Verb	*Adverb*
acted	quickly, suddenly, warily
ate	greedily, hungrily, quickly
bled	freely, profusely, slightly
explained	briefly, quickly, clearly
decided	carefully, eventually, immediately
fought	bravely, furiously, gamely
left	hurriedly, quietly, suddenly
lost	badly, heavily, sportingly
pulled	strongly, vigorously
ran	hurriedly, quickly, rapidly, slowly
remembered	clearly, distinctly, faintly
sang	loudly, sweetly, tunefully
smiled	broadly, happily
spent	foolishly, recklessly, sparingly, freely
spoke	softly, clearly distinctly, earnestly, loudly, plainly, slowly
trembled	awkwardly, drunkenly, weakly
waited	patiently, anxiously
walked	clumsily, haltingly, quickly, sadly
whispered	softly, audibly, quietly
shouted	frantically, joyfully, soundly

Some Descriptive Adverbial and Adjectival Phrases for Expressing Feelings
- My heart was in my mouth.
- My feet were rooted to the spot.
- My throat was so dry, I wasn't able to utter a single word.
- I was breathing hard and fast.
- My body was shaking as if I were operating a drill.
- I screamed in terror.
- My mouth fell open in surprise and fear.
- I waited nervously.
- He gave out an ear-piercing cry.

Examples of General Expressions
- He could not believe what was happening, but before long he gained his composure.
- A hearty smile a crossed the man's lips.
- The news left her numb, but then she went wild with joy.
- The crowd went wild, clapping, cheering, and yelling.
- He was overwhelmed and filled with joy.

- She shed tears of joy.
- She shed crocodile tears. (She pretended.)
- I had scarcely … before …
- No sooner had … than …
- My throat was so parched, I could have drunk dish water.
- My joy knew no bounds.
- He suspected that the thieves might be attracted to our home, so we stayed up the whole night.

Printed in the United States
By Bookmasters